Doctrinal Standards

and Our
Theological
Task

The Book of Discipline of The
United Methodist Church

PART II

DOCTRINAL STANDARDS
AND
OUR THEOLOGICAL TASK

Student Book
(ISBN: 0-687-75442-9)
Copyright © 1989 by Graded Press

An official resource for The United
Methodist Church prepared by the
General Board of Discipleship
through the Division of Church
School Publications and published
by Graded Press, a division of The
United Methodist Publishing
House; 201 Eighth Avenue, South;
P.O. Box 801; Nashville, TN 37202.
Printed in the United States of
America.

Contents

A Message From the

 **Council of Bishops** THE UNITED METHODIST CHURCH

The 1988 Session of the General Conference of The United Methodist Church asked the Council of Bishops to lead a denomination-wide study of the theological documents contained in Part II of the 1988 *Book of Discipline*.

This reprint of Part II is one resource for that study. Any form of study must begin with this primary document.

A thirteen-session leader's guide is available as a companion piece for this reprint. Other study materials also will be prepared for various settings.

It is the hope of the Council of Bishops that every United Methodist will become acquainted with this document and that as many as possible of our members and constituents will study it, either individually or in some organized group.

Such a study should clarify our identity as United Methodists and thus enable us better to fulfill our role and mission within the total Christian community.

Leroy C. Hodapp, Chair
Standing Committee on Teaching Concerns
United Methodist Council of Bishops

Part II
DOCTRINAL STANDARDS AND OUR THEOLOGICAL TASK[1]

¶ 66. SECTION 1—OUR DOCTRINAL HERITAGE

United Methodists profess the historic Christian faith in God, incarnate in Jesus Christ for our salvation and ever at work in human history in the Holy Spirit. Living in a covenant of grace under the Lordship of Jesus Christ, we participate in the first fruits of God's coming reign and pray in hope for its full realization on earth as in heaven.

Our heritage in doctrine and our present theological task focus upon a renewed grasp of the sovereignty of God and of God's love in Christ amid the continuing crises of human existence.

Our forebears in the faith reaffirmed the ancient Christian message as found in the apostolic witness, even as they applied it anew in their own circumstances.

Their preaching and teaching were grounded in Scripture, informed by Christian tradition, enlivened in experience, and tested by reason.

Their labors inspire and inform our attempts to convey the saving gospel to our world with its needs and aspirations.

---

[1]The Judicial Council ruled in 1972 that all sections of Part II except ¶ 68 were "legislative enactments and neither part of the Constitution nor under the Restrictive Rules" (*See* Judicial Council Decision 358).

Our Common Heritage as Christians

United Methodists share a common heritage with Christians of every age and nation. This heritage is grounded in the apostolic witness to Jesus Christ as Savior and Lord, which is the source and measure of all valid Christian teaching.

Faced with diverse interpretations of the apostolic message, leaders of the early church sought to specify the core of Christian belief in order to ensure the soundness of Christian teaching.

The determination of the canon of Christian Scripture and the adoption of ecumenical creeds, such as the formulations of Nicaea and Chalcedon, were of central importance to this consensual process. Such creeds helped preserve the integrity of the Church's witness, set boundaries for acceptable Christian doctrine, and proclaimed the basic elements of the enduring Christian message. These statements of faith, along with the Apostles' Creed, contain the most prominent features of our ecumenical heritage.

The Protestant reformers of the sixteenth and seventeenth centuries devised new confessional statements that reiterated classical Christian teaching in an attempt to recover the authentic biblical witness. These documents affirmed the primacy of Scripture and provided formal doctrinal standards through their statements of essential beliefs on matters such as the way of salvation, the Christian life, and the nature of the Church.

Many distinctively Protestant teachings were transmitted into United Methodist understandings through doctrinal formulations such as the Articles of Religion of the Church of England and the Heidelberg Catechism of the Reformed tradition.

Various doctrinal statements in the form of creeds, confessions of belief, and articles of faith were officially adopted by churches as standards of Christian teaching. Notwithstanding their importance, these formal doctrinal standards by no means exhausted authoritative Christian teaching.

The standards themselves initially emerged from a much wider body of Christian thought and practice, and their fuller significance unfolded in the writings of the Church's teachers.

7

Some writings have proved simply to be dated benchmarks in the story of the Church's continuing maturation.

By contrast, some sermons, treatises, liturgies, and hymns have gained considerable practical authority in the life and thought of the Church by virtue of their wide and continuing acceptance as faithful expositions of Christian teaching. Nonetheless, the basic measure of authenticity in doctrinal standards, whether formally established or received by tradition, has been their fidelity to the apostolic faith grounded in Scripture and evidenced in the life of the Church through the centuries.

Basic Christian Affirmations

With Christians of other communions we confess belief in the triune God—Father, Son, and Holy Spirit. This confession embraces the biblical witness to God's activity in creation, encompasses God's gracious self-involvement in the dramas of history, and anticipates the consummation of God's reign.

The created order is designed for the well-being of all creatures and as the place of human dwelling in covenant with God. As sinful creatures, however, we have broken that covenant, become estranged from God, wounded ourselves and one another, and wreaked havoc throughout the natural order. We stand in need of redemption.

We hold in common with all Christians a faith in the mystery of salvation in and through Jesus Christ. At the heart of the gospel of salvation is God's incarnation in Jesus of Nazareth. Scripture witnesses to the redeeming love of God in Jesus' life and teachings, his atoning death, his resurrection, his sovereign presence in history, his triumph over the powers of evil and death, and his promised return. Because God truly loves us in spite of our willful sin, God judges us, summons us to repentance, pardons us, receives us by that grace given to us in Jesus Christ, and gives us hope of life eternal.

We share the Christian belief that God's redemptive love is realized in human life by the activity of the Holy Spirit, both in personal experience and in the community of believers. This community is the Church, which the Spirit has brought into existence for the healing of the nations.

Through faith in Jesus Christ we are forgiven, reconciled to God, and transformed as people of the new covenant.

"Life in the Spirit" involves diligent use of the means of grace such as praying, fasting, attending upon the Sacraments, and inward searching in solitude. It also encompasses the communal life of the Church in worship, mission, evangelism, service, and social witness.

We understand ourselves to be part of Christ's universal Church when by adoration, proclamation, and service we become conformed to Christ. We are initiated and incorporated into this community of faith by Baptism, receiving the promise of the Spirit that re-creates and transforms us. Through the regular celebration of Holy Communion, we participate in the risen presence of Jesus Christ and are thereby nourished for faithful discipleship.

We pray and work for the coming of God's realm and reign to the world and rejoice in the promise of everlasting life that overcomes death and the forces of evil.

With other Christians we recognize that the reign of God is both a present and future reality. The Church is called to be that place where the first signs of the reign of God are identified and acknowledged in the world. Wherever persons are being made new creatures in Christ, wherever the insights and resources of the gospel are brought to bear on the life of the world, God's reign is already effective in its healing and renewing power.

We also look to the end time in which God's work will be fulfilled. This prospect gives us hope in our present actions, as individuals and as the Church. This expectation saves us from resignation and motivates our continuing witness and service.

We share with many Christian communions a recognition of the authority of Scripture in matters of faith, the confession that our justification as sinners is by grace through faith, and the sober realization that the Church is in need of continual reformation and renewal.

We affirm the general ministry of all baptized Christians who share responsibility for building up the Church and reaching out in mission and service to the world.

With other Christians, we declare the essential oneness of the Church in Christ Jesus. This rich heritage of shared Christian belief finds expression in our hymnody and liturgies. Our unity is affirmed in the historic creeds as we confess one holy, catholic, and apostolic Church. It is also experienced in joint ventures of ministry and in various forms of ecumenical cooperation.

Nourished by common roots of this shared Christian heritage, the branches of Christ's Church have developed diverse traditions that enlarge our store of shared understandings. Our avowed ecumenical commitment as United Methodists is to gather our own doctrinal emphases into the larger Christian unity, there to be made more meaningful in a richer whole.

If we are to offer our best gifts to the common Christian treasury, we must make a deliberate effort as a church to strive for critical self-understanding. It is as Christians involved in ecumenical partnership that we embrace and examine our distinctive heritage.

Our Distinctive Heritage as United Methodists

The underlying energy of the Wesleyan theological heritage stems from an emphasis upon practical divinity, the implementation of genuine Christianity in the lives of believers.

Methodism did not arise in response to a specific doctrinal dispute, though there was no lack of theological controversy. Early Methodists claimed to preach the scriptural doctrines of the Church of England as contained in the Articles of Religion, the Homilies, and the Book of Common Prayer.

Their task was not to reformulate doctrine. Their tasks were to summon people to experience the justifying and sanctifying grace of God and encourage people to grow in the knowledge and love of God through the personal and corporate disciplines of the Christian life.

The thrust of the Wesleyan movement and of the United Brethren and Evangelical Association was "to reform the nation, particularly the Church, and to spread scriptural holiness over the land."

Wesley's orientation toward the practical is evident in his focus upon the "scripture way of salvation." He considered doctrinal matters primarily in terms of their significance for Christian discipleship.

The Wesleyan emphasis upon the Christian life—faith and love put into practice—has been the hallmark of those traditions now incorporated into The United Methodist Church. The distinctive shape of the Wesleyan theological heritage can be seen in a constellation of doctrinal emphases that display the creating, redeeming, and sanctifying activity of God.

Distinctive Wesleyan Emphases

Although Wesley shared with many other Christians a belief in grace, justification, assurance, and sanctification, he combined them in a powerful manner to create distinctive emphases for living the full Christian life. The Evangelical United Brethren tradition, particularly as expressed by Phillip William Otterbein, from a Reformed background, gave similar distinctive emphases.

Grace pervades our understanding of Christian faith and life. By grace we mean the undeserved, unmerited, and loving action of God in human existence through the ever-present Holy Spirit. While the grace of God is undivided, it precedes salvation as "prevenient grace," continues in "justifying grace," and is brought to fruition in "sanctifying grace."

We assert that God's grace is manifest in all creation even though suffering, violence, and evil are everywhere present. The goodness of creation is fulfilled in human beings, who are called to covenant partnership with God. God has endowed us with dignity and freedom and has summoned us to responsibility for our lives and the life of the world.

In God's self-revelation, Jesus Christ, we see the splendor of our true humanity. Even our sin, with its destructive conse-

11

quences for all creation, does not alter God's intention for us—holiness and happiness of heart. Nor does it diminish our accountability for the way we live.

Despite our brokenness, we remain creatures brought into being by a just and merciful God. The restoration of God's image in our lives requires divine grace to renew our fallen nature.

Prevenient Grace.—We acknowledge God's prevenient grace, the divine love that surrounds all humanity and precedes any and all of our conscious impulses. This grace prompts our first wish to please God, our first glimmer of understanding concerning God's will, and our "first slight transient conviction" of having sinned against God.

God's grace also awakens in us an earnest longing for deliverance from sin and death and moves us toward repentance and faith.

Justification and Assurance.—We believe God reaches out to the repentant believer in justifying grace with accepting and pardoning love. Wesleyan theology stresses that a decisive change in the human heart can and does occur under the prompting of grace and the guidance of the Holy Spirit.

In justification we are, through faith, forgiven our sin and restored to God's favor. This righting of relationships by God through Christ calls forth our faith and trust as we experience regeneration, by which we are made new creatures in Christ.

This process of justification and new birth is often referred to as conversion. Such a change may be sudden and dramatic, or gradual and cumulative. It marks a new beginning, yet it is part of an ongoing process. Christian experience as personal transformation always expresses itself as faith working by love.

Our Wesleyan theology also embraces the scriptural promise that we can expect to receive assurance of our present salvation, as the Spirit "bears witness with our spirit that we are children of God."

Sanctification and Perfection.—We hold that the wonder of God's acceptance and pardon does not end God's saving work, which continues to nurture our growth in grace. Through the power of the Holy Spirit we are enabled to increase in the knowledge and love of God and in love for our neighbor.

New birth is the first step in this process of sanctification. Sanctifying grace draws us toward the gift of Christian perfection, which Wesley described as a heart "habitually filled with the love of God and neighbor" and as "having the mind of Christ and walking as he walked."

This gracious gift of God's power and love, the hope and expectation of the faithful, is neither warranted by our efforts nor limited by our frailties.

Faith and Good Works.—We see God's grace and human activity working together in the relationship of faith and good works. God's grace calls forth human response and discipline.

Faith is the only response essential for salvation. However, the General Rules remind us that salvation evidences itself in good works. For Wesley, even repentance should be accompanied by "fruits meet for repentance," or works of piety and mercy.

Both faith and good works belong within an all-encompassing theology of grace, since they stem from God's gracious love "shed abroad in our hearts by the Holy Spirit."

Mission and Service.—We insist that personal salvation always involves Christian mission and service to the world. By joining heart and hand we assert that personal religion, evangelical witness, and Christian social action are reciprocal and mutually reinforcing.

Scriptural holiness entails more than personal piety; love of God is always linked with love of neighbor, a passion for justice and renewal in the life of the world.

The General Rules represent one traditional expression of the intrinsic relationship between Christian life and thought as understood within the Wesleyan tradition. Theology is the servant of piety, which in turn is the ground of social conscience and the impetus for social action and global interaction, always in the empowering context of the reign of God.

Nurture and Mission of the Church.—Finally, we emphasize the nurturing and serving function of Christian fellowship in the

Church. The personal experience of faith is nourished by the worshiping community.

For Wesley there is no religion but social religion, no holiness but social holiness. The communal forms of faith in the Wesleyan tradition not only promote personal growth; they also equip and mobilize us for mission and service to the world.

The outreach of the Church springs from the working of the Spirit. As United Methodists, we respond to that working through a connectional polity based upon mutual responsiveness and accountability. Connectional ties bind us together in faith and service in our global witness, enabling faith to become active in love and intensifying our desire for peace and justice in the world.

Doctrine and Discipline in the Christian Life

No motif in the Wesleyan tradition has been more constant than the link between Christian doctrine and Christian living. Methodists have always been strictly enjoined to maintain the unity of faith and good works through the means of grace, as seen in John Wesley's *The Nature, Design, and General Rules of the United Societies* (1743). The coherence of faith with ministries of love forms the discipline of Wesleyan spirituality and Christian discipleship.

The General Rules were originally designed for members of Methodist societies, who participated in the sacramental life of the Church of England. The terms of membership in these societies were simple: "a desire to flee from the wrath to come and to be saved from their sins."

Wesley insisted, however, that evangelical faith should manifest itself in evangelical living. He spelled out this expectation in the three-part formula of the Rules:

It is therefore expected of all who continue therein that they should continue to evidence their desire of salvation,
First: By doing no harm, by avoiding evil of every kind . . . ;
Secondly: By . . . doing good of every possible sort, and, as far as possible, to all . . . ;
Thirdly: By attending upon all the ordinances of God (*See* ¶ 68).

Wesley's illustrative cases under each of these three rules show how the Christian conscience might move from general principles to specific actions. Their explicit combination highlights the spiritual spring of moral action.

Wesley rejected undue reliance upon these rules. Discipline was not church law; it was a way of discipleship. Wesley insisted that true religion is "the knowledge of God in Christ Jesus," "the life which is hid with Christ in God," and "the righteousness that [the true believer] thirsts after."

General Rules and Social Principles

Upon such evangelical premises, Methodists in every age have sought to exercise their responsibility for the moral and spiritual quality of society. In asserting the connection between doctrine and ethics, the General Rules provide an early signal of Methodist social consciousness.

The Social Principles (¶¶ 70-76) provide our most recent official summary of stated convictions that seek to apply the Christian vision of righteousness to social, economic, and political issues. Our historic opposition to evils such as smuggling, inhumane prison conditions, slavery, drunkenness, and child labor was founded upon a vivid sense of God's wrath against human injustice and wastage.

Our struggles for human dignity and social reform have been a response to God's demand for love, mercy, and justice in the light of the Kingdom. We proclaim no *personal gospel* that fails to express itself in relevant social concerns; we proclaim no *social gospel* that does not include the personal transformation of sinners.

It is our conviction that the good news of the Kingdom must judge, redeem, and reform the sinful social structures of our time.

The Book of Discipline and the General Rules convey the expectation of discipline within the experience of individuals and the life of the Church. Such discipline assumes accountability to the community of faith by those who claim that community's support.

Support without accountability promotes moral weakness; accountability without support is a form of cruelty.

A church that rushes to punishment is not open to God's mercy, but a church lacking the courage to act decisively on personal and social issues loses its claim to moral authority. The Church exercises its discipline as a community through which God continues to "reconcile the world to himself."

Conclusion

These distinctive emphases of United Methodists provide the basis for "practical divinity," the experiential realization of the gospel of Jesus Christ in the lives of Christian people. These emphases have been preserved not so much through formal doctrinal declarations as through the vital movement of faith and practice as seen in converted lives and within the disciplined life of the Church.

Devising formal definitions of doctrine has been less pressing for United Methodists than summoning people to faith and nurturing them in the knowledge and love of God. The core of Wesleyan doctrine that informed our past rightly belongs to our common heritage as Christians and remains a prime component within our continuing theological task.

¶ 67. SECTION 2—OUR DOCTRINAL HISTORY

The pioneers in the traditions that flowed together into The United Methodist Church understood themselves as standing in the central stream of Christian spirituality and doctrine, loyal heirs of the authentic Christian tradition. In John Wesley's words, theirs was "the old religion, the religion of the Bible, the religion . . . of the whole church in the purest ages." Their gospel was grounded in the biblical message of God's self-giving love revealed in Jesus Christ.

Wesley's portrayal of the spiritual pilgrimage in terms of "the scripture way of salvation" provided their model for experiential Christianity. They assumed and insisted upon the integrity of basic Christian truth and emphasized its practical application in the lives of believers.

This perspective is apparent in the Wesleyan understanding of "catholic spirit." While it is true that United Methodists are fixed upon certain religious affirmations, grounded in the gospel and confirmed in their experience, they also recognize the right of Christians to disagree on matters such as forms of worship, structures of church government, modes of Baptism, or theological explorations. They believe such differences do not break the bond of fellowship that ties Christians together in Jesus Christ. Wesley's familiar dictum was, "As to all opinions which do not strike at the root of Christianity, we think and let think."

But, even as they were fully committed to the principles of religious toleration and theological diversity they were equally confident that there is a "marrow" of Christian truth that can be identified and that must be conserved. This living core, as they believed, stands revealed in Scripture, illumined by tradition, vivified in personal and corporate experience, and confirmed by reason. They were very much aware, of course, that God's eternal Word never has been, nor can be, exhaustively expressed in any single form of words.

They were also prepared, as a matter of course, to reaffirm the ancient creeds and confessions as valid summaries of Christian truth. But they were careful not to set them apart as absolute standards for doctrinal truth and error.

Beyond the essentials of vital religion, United Methodists respect the diversity of opinions held by conscientious persons of faith. Wesley followed a time-tested approach: "In essentials, unity; in non-essentials, liberty; and in all things, charity."

The spirit of charity takes into consideration the limits of human understanding. "To be ignorant of many things and to be mistaken in some," Wesley observed, "is the necessary condition of humanity." The crucial matter in religion is steadfast love for God and neighbor, empowered by the redeeming and sanctifying work of the Holy Spirit.

The Wesleyan "Standards" in Great Britain

In this spirit, the British Methodists under the Wesleys never reduced their theology to a confessional formula as a doctrinal test. Methodism was a movement within the Church of England, and John Wesley constantly maintained that he taught the scriptural doctrines contained in the Thirty-Nine Articles, the Homilies, and the Book of Common Prayer of his national church. The Bible, of course, constituted for him the final authority in all doctrinal matters.

As the movement grew, Wesley provided his people with published sermons and a Bible commentary for their doctrinal instruction. His *Sermons on Several Occasions* (1746–60) set forth those doctrines which, he said, "I embrace and teach as the essentials of true religion." In 1755, he published *Explanatory Notes Upon the New Testament* as a guide for Methodist biblical exegesis and doctrinal interpretation.

As occasional controversies arose, the need for a standard measure of Methodist preaching became evident. In 1763, Wesley produced a "Model Deed" for Methodist properties, which stipulated that the trustees for each preaching house were responsible for ensuring that the preachers in their pulpits "preach no other doctrine than is contained in Mr. Wesley's *Notes Upon the New Testament* and four volumes of *Sermons.*"

These writings, then, contained the standard exposition of Methodist teaching. They provide a model and measure for adequate preaching in the Wesleyan tradition. The primary norm for Wesley's writings was Scripture, as illumined by historic traditions and vital faith. Wesley put forth no summary of biblical revelation for the British Methodists because the Thirty-Nine Articles of the Church of England were already available.

The Wesley brothers also composed hymns that were rich in doctrinal and experiential content. The hymns, especially those of Charles Wesley, not only are among the best-loved within Methodism but also are major resources for doctrinal instruction.

Furthermore, John Wesley specified various disciplines and rules, such as the General Rules, to implement in personal and communal life the practical divinity he proclaimed.

In addition to these writings, Wesley established the conference to instruct and supervise the Methodist preachers. He produced Minutes to ensure their fidelity to the doctrines and disciplines of the Methodist movement. These writings and structures filled out the Wesleyan understanding of the Church and the Christian life.

Doctrinal Standards in American Methodism

As long as the American colonies were primarily under British control, the Methodists could continue as part of the sacramental community of the Church of England. The early conferences, under the leadership of British preachers, declared their allegiance to the Wesleyan principles of organization and doctrine. They stipulated that the Minutes of the British and American conferences, along with the *Sermons* and *Notes* of Wesley, contained their basic doctrine and discipline.

After the formal recognition of American independence in 1783, Wesley realized that the Methodists in America were free of English control, religious as well as civil, and should become an independent Methodist church. Wesley then furnished the American Methodists with a liturgy *(The Sunday Service of the Methodists in North America)* and a doctrinal statement *(The Articles of Religion)*. The Sunday Service was Wesley's abridgment of the Book of Common Prayer; the Articles of Religion were his revision of the Thirty-Nine Articles.

The American Methodist preachers, gathered at Baltimore in December 1784, adopted the Sunday Service and the Articles of Religion as part of their actions in forming the new Methodist Episcopal Church. This "Christmas Conference" also accepted a hymnbook that Wesley had prepared (1784) and adopted a slightly modified version of the General Rules as a statement of the Church's nature and discipline. The conference spent most of its time adapting the British "Large Minutes" to American conditions. Subsequent editions of this document came to be known as the *Doctrines and Discipline of the Methodist Episcopal Church* (the Book of Discipline).

The shift from "movement" to "church" had changed the function of doctrinal norms within American Methodism. Rather than prescribing doctrinal emphases for preaching within a movement, the Articles outlined basic norms for Christian belief within a church, following the traditional Anglican fashion.

The preface to the first separate publication of the Articles states, "These are the doctrines taught among the people called Methodists. Nor is there any doctrine whatever, generally

19

received among that people, contrary to the articles now before you."

American Methodists were not required to subscribe to the Articles after the Anglican manner, but they were accountable (under threat of trial) for keeping their proclamation of the gospel within the boundaries outlined therein. For generations, the *Doctrines and Discipline* cited only the Articles as the basis for testing correct doctrine in the newly formed Church: the charge of doctrinal irregularity against preachers or members was for "disseminating doctrines contrary to our Articles of Religion." In this manner, the Church protected its doctrinal integrity against the heresies that were prevalent at the time—Socinianism, Arianism, and Pelagianism (*see* Articles I, II, and IX).

The Articles of Religion, however, did not guarantee adequate Methodist preaching; they lacked several Wesleyan emphases, such as assurance and Christian perfection. Wesley's *Sermons* and *Notes*, therefore, continued to function as the traditional standard exposition of distinctive Methodist teaching.

The General Conference of 1808, which provided the first Constitution of the Methodist Episcopal Church, established the Articles of Religion as the Church's explicit doctrinal standards. The first Restrictive Rule of the Constitution prohibited any change, alteration, or addition to the Articles themselves, and it stipulated that no new standards or rules of doctrine could be adopted that were contrary to the "present existing and established standards of doctrine."

Within the Wesleyan tradition, then as now, the *Sermons* and *Notes* furnished models of doctrinal exposition. Other documents have also served American Methodism as vital expressions of Methodist teaching and preaching. Lists of recommended doctrinal resources vary from generation to generation but generally acknowledge the importance of the hymnbook, the ecumenical creeds, and the General Rules. Lists of such writings in the early nineteenth century usually included John Fletcher's *Checks Against Antinomianism* and Richard Watson's *Theological Institutes*.

The doctrinal emphases of these statements were carried forward by the weight of tradition rather than the force of law.

They became part of the heritage of American Methodism to the degree that they remained useful to continuing generations.

During the great frontier revivals of the nineteenth century, the influence of European theological traditions waned in America. Preaching focused on "Christian experience," understood chiefly as "saving faith in Christ." Among the Methodists there was a consistent stress on free will, infant baptism, and informal worship, which led to protracted controversies with the Presbyterians, Baptists, and Episcopalians, respectively.

Methodist interest in formal doctrinal standards remained secondary to evangelism, nurture, and mission. The Wesleyan hymnody served in practice as the most important single means of communicating and preserving the doctrinal substance of the gospel.

By the end of the nineteenth century, Methodist theology in America had become decidedly eclectic, with less specific attention paid to its Wesleyan sources.

The force of the Articles of Religion underwent several shifts. For a time, the first Restrictive Rule was exempted from the process of constitutional amendment, thus allowing no consideration of change in doctrinal standards. Mention of the Articles of Religion was included in the membership vows of the Methodist Episcopal Church, South.

At the beginning of the twentieth century, however, the waning force of doctrinal discipline and the decreasing influence of the Wesleyan theological heritage among the American Methodists, along with minor but significant changes in the wording of the Book of Discipline regarding doctrinal standards, led to a steady dilution of the force of the Articles of Religion as the Church's constitutional standards of doctrine.

During this same period, theologians and church leaders began to explore ways of expressing the gospel that were in keeping with developing intellectual currents. These leaders also began to rethink the historical social compassion of the Wesleyan tradition in the midst of the emerging industrial, urban civilization. They deepened our awareness of the systemic nature of evil and the urgency to proclaim the gospel promise of social redemption. Consequently, theologies supportive of the social gospel found fertile soil within the Methodist traditions.

These years were times of theological and ethical controversy within Methodism as new patterns of thought clashed with the more familiar themes and styles of the previous two centuries.

In recent decades there has been a strong recovery of interest in Wesley and in the more classic traditions of Christian thought. This recovery has been part of a broad resurgence of Reformation theology and practice in Europe and America, renewing the historical legacy of Protestantism in the context of the modern world. These trends have been reinforced in North America by the reaffirmation of evangelical piety.

The ecumenical movement has brought new appreciation for the unity as well as the richness and diversity of the Church catholic.

Currents of theology have developed out of black people's struggle for freedom, the movement for the full equality of women in Church and society, and the quest for liberation and for indigenous forms of Christian existence in churches around the world.

The challenge to United Methodists is to discern the various strands of these vital movements of faith that are coherent, faithful understandings of the gospel and the Christian mission for our times.

The task of defining the scope of our Wesleyan tradition in the context of the contemporary world includes much more than formally reaffirming or redefining standards of doctrine, although these tasks may also be involved. The heart of our task is to reclaim and renew the distinctive United Methodist doctrinal heritage, which rightly belongs to our common heritage as Christians, for the life and mission of the whole Church today.

Doctrinal Traditions in the Evangelical Church and the United Brethren Church

The unfolding of doctrinal concerns among Jacob Albright's Evangelical Association and Phillip William Otterbein's United Brethren in Christ roughly parallels Methodist developments. Differences emerged largely from differing ecclesiastical traditions brought from Germany and Holland, together with the modified Calvinism of the Heidelberg Catechism.

In the German-speaking communities of America, Albright and Otterbein considered evangelism more important than theological speculation. Although they were not doctrinally indifferent, they stressed conversion, "justification by faith confirmed by a sensible assurance thereof," Christian nurture, the priesthood of all believers in a shared ministry of Christian witness and service, and entire sanctification as the goal of Christian life.

As with Wesley, their primary source and norm for Christian teaching was Scripture. Otterbein enjoined his followers "to be careful to preach no other doctrine than what is plainly laid down in the Bible." Each new member was asked "to confess that he received the Bible as the Word of God." Ordinands were required to affirm without reserve the plenary authority of Scripture.

Matched with these affirmations was the conviction that converted Christians are enabled by the Holy Spirit to read Scripture with a special Christian consciousness. They prized this principle as the supreme guide in biblical interpretation.

Jacob Albright was directed by the Conference of 1807 to prepare a list of Articles of Religion. He died before he could attempt the task.

George Miller then assumed the responsibility. He recommended to the Conference of 1809 the adoption of the German translation of the Methodist Articles of Religion, with the addition of a new one, "Of the Last Judgment." The recommendation was adopted. This action affirms a conscious choice of the Methodist Articles as normative. The added article was from the Augsburg Confession, on a theme omitted in the Anglican Articles.

In 1816, the original twenty-six Articles were reduced to twenty-one by omitting five polemical articles aimed at Roman Catholics, Anabaptists, and sixteenth-century sectaries. This act of deletion reflected a conciliatory spirit in a time of bitter controversy.

In 1839, a few slight changes were made in the text of 1816. It was then stipulated that "the Articles of Faith . . . should be constitutionally unchangeable among us."

In the 1870s, a proposal to revise the Articles touched off a flurry of debate, but the Conference of 1875 decisively rejected the proposal.

In later action the twenty-one Articles were reduced to nineteen by combining several, but without omitting any of their original content.

These nineteen were brought intact into the Evangelical United Brethren union of 1946.

Among the United Brethren in Christ, a summary of normative teaching was formulated in 1813 by Christian Newcomer and Christopher Grosch, colleagues of Otterbein. Its first three paragraphs follow the order of the Apostles' Creed. Paragraphs four and five affirm the primacy of Scripture and the universal proclamation of "the biblical doctrine . . . of man's fall in Adam and his deliverance through Jesus Christ." An added section commends "the ordinances of baptism and the remembrance of the Lord" and approves foot washing as optional.

The first General Conference of the United Brethren in Christ (1815) adopted a slight revision of this earlier statement as the denomination's Confession of Faith. A further revision was made in 1841, with the stipulation that there be no further changes: "No rule or ordinance shall at any time be passed to change or do away with the Confession of Faith as it now stands." Even so, agitation for change continued.

In 1885, a church commission was appointed to "prepare such a form of belief and such amended fundamental rules for the government of this church in the future as will, in their judgment, be best adapted to secure its growth and efficiency in the work of evangelizing the world."

The resulting proposal for a new Confession of Faith and Constitution was submitted to the general membership of the Church, the first such referendum on a Confession of Faith in United Brethren history, and was then placed before the General Conference of 1889. Both the general membership and the Conference approved the Confession by preponderant majorities. It was thereupon enacted by episcopal "proclamation." However, this action was protested by a minority as a violation of the Restrictive Rule of 1841 and became a basic cause for a consequent schism, resulting in the formation of The United Brethren Church (Old Constitution).

The Confession of Faith of 1889 was more comprehensive than any of its antecedents, with articles on depravity, justification, regeneration and adoption, sanctification, the Christian Sabbath, and the future state. The article on sanctification, though brief, is significant in its reflection of the doctrine of holiness of the Heidelberg Catechism. The 1889 Confession was brought by the United Brethren into the union with the Evangelicals in 1946.

The Evangelical United Brethren Confession of Faith

The Discipline of the new Evangelical United Brethren Church (1946) contained both the Evangelical Articles and the United Brethren Confession. Twelve years later the General Conference of the united church authorized its Board of Bishops to prepare a new Confession of Faith.

A new Confession, with sixteen articles, of a somewhat more modern character than any of its antecedents, was presented to the General Conference of 1962 and adopted without amendment. The Evangelical article, "Entire Sanctification and Christian Perfection," is reflected in this confession as a distinctive emphasis. The Confession of Faith replaced both former Articles and Confession and was brought over intact into the Discipline of The United Methodist Church (1968).

Doctrinal Standards in The United Methodist Church

In the Plan of Union for The United Methodist Church, the preface to the Methodist Articles of Religion and the Evangelical United Brethren Confession of Faith explains that both were accepted as doctrinal standards for the new Church. Additionally, it stated that although the language of the first Restrictive Rule never has been formally defined, Wesley's *Sermons* and *Notes* were understood specifically to be included in our present existing and established standards of doctrine. It also stated that the Articles, the Confession, and the Wesleyan "standards" were "thus deemed congruent if not identical in their doctrinal perspectives

25

and not in conflict." This declaration was accepted by subsequent rulings of the Judicial Council.[2]

The Constitution of The United Methodist Church, in its Restrictive Rules (*see* ¶¶ 16-20), protects both the Articles of Religion and the Confession of Faith as doctrinal standards that shall not be revoked, altered, or changed. The process of creating new "standards or rules of doctrine" thus continues to be restricted, requiring either that they be declared "not contrary to" the present standards or that they go through the difficult process of constitutional amendment.

The United Methodist Church stands continually in need of doctrinal reinvigoration for the sake of authentic renewal, fruitful evangelism, and ecumenical dialogue. In this light, the recovery and updating of our distinctive doctrinal heritage—catholic, evangelical, and reformed—is essential.[3]

This task calls for the repossession of our traditions as well as the promotion of theological inquiry both within the denomination and in our ecumenical efforts. All are invited to share in this endeavor to stimulate an active interest in doctrinal understanding in order to claim our legacy and to shape that legacy for the Church we aspire to be.

¶ 68. SECTION 3—OUR DOCTRINAL STANDARDS AND GENERAL RULES

THE ARTICLES OF RELIGION OF THE METHODIST CHURCH[4]

[Bibliographical Note: The Articles of Religion are here reprinted from the *Discipline* of 1808 (when the first Restrictive Rule took effect), collated against Wesely's original text in *The Sunday Service of the Methodists* (1784). To these are added two Articles: "Of Sanctification" and "Of the Duty of Christians to the Civil Authority," which are legislative enactments and not integral parts of the document as protected by the Constitution (*see* Judicial Council Decisions 41, 176).]

---

[2]*See* Judicial Council Decision 358.

[3]The need to interpret the Articles in the light of their historical context and biases is reflected in the Resolution of Intent (1970), found in the Book of Resolutions.

[4]Protected by Restrictive Rule 1 (¶ 16).

Article I.—Of Faith in the Holy Trinity

There is but one living and true God, everlasting, without body or parts, of infinite power, wisdom, and goodness; the maker and preserver of all things, both visible and invisible. And in unity of this Godhead there are three persons, of one substance, power, and eternity—the Father, the Son, and the Holy Ghost.

Article II.—Of the Word, or Son of God, Who Was Made Very Man

The Son, who is the Word of the Father, the very and eternal God, of one substance with the Father, took man's nature in the womb of the blessed Virgin; so that two whole and perfect natures, that is to say, the Godhead and Manhood, were joined together in one person, never to be divided; whereof is one Christ, very God and very Man, who truly suffered, was crucified, dead, and buried, to reconcile his Father to us, and to be a sacrifice, not only for original guilt, but also for actual sins of men.

Article III.—Of the Resurrection of Christ

Christ did truly rise again from the dead, and took again his body, with all things appertaining to the perfection of man's nature, wherewith he ascended into heaven, and there sitteth until he return to judge all men at the last day.

Article IV.—Of the Holy Ghost

The Holy Ghost, proceeding from the Father and the Son, is of one substance, majesty, and glory with the Father and the Son, very and eternal God.

Article V.—Of the Sufficiency of the Holy Scriptures for Salvation

The Holy Scripture containeth all things necessary to salvation; so that whatsoever is not read therein, nor may be

27

proved thereby, is not to be required of any man that it should be believed as an article of faith, or be thought requisite or necessary to salvation. In the name of the Holy Scripture we do understand those canonical books of the Old and New Testament of whose authority was never any doubt in the Church. The names of the canonical books are:

Genesis, Exodus, Leviticus, Numbers, Deuteronomy, Joshua, Judges, Ruth, The First Book of Samuel, The Second Book of Samuel, The First Book of Kings, The Second Book of Kings, The First Book of Chronicles, The Second Book of Chronicles, The Book of Ezra, The Book of Nehemiah, The Book of Esther, The Book of Job, The Psalms, The Proverbs, Ecclesiastes or the Preacher, Cantica or Songs of Solomon, Four Prophets the Greater, Twelve Prophets the Less.

All the books of the New Testament, as they are commonly received, we do receive and account canonical.

Article VI.—Of the Old Testament

The Old Testament is not contrary to the New; for both in the Old and New Testament everlasting life is offered to mankind by Christ, who is the only Mediator between God and man, being both God and Man. Wherefore they are not to be heard who feign that the old fathers did look only for transitory promises. Although the law given from God by Moses as touching ceremonies and rites doth not bind Christians, nor ought the civil precepts thereof of necessity be received in any commonwealth; yet notwithstanding, no Christian whatsoever is free from the obedience of the commandments which are called moral.

Article VII.—Of Original or Birth Sin

Original sin standeth not in the following of Adam (as the Pelagians do vainly talk), but it is the corruption of the nature of every man, that naturally is engendered of the offspring of Adam, whereby man is very far gone from original righteousness, and of his own nature inclined to evil, and that continually.

Article VIII.—Of Free Will

The condition of man after the fall of Adam is such that he cannot turn and prepare himself, by his own natural strength and works, to faith, and calling upon God; wherefore we have no power to do good works, pleasant and acceptable to God, without the grace of God by Christ preventing us, that we may have a good will, and working with us, when we have that good will.

Article IX.—Of the Justification of Man

We are accounted righteous before God only for the merit of our Lord and Saviour Jesus Christ, by faith, and not for our own works or deservings. Wherefore, that we are justified by faith, only, is a most wholesome doctrine, and very full of comfort.

Article X.—Of Good Works

Although good works, which are the fruits of faith, and follow after justification, cannot put away our sins, and endure the severity of God's judgment; yet are they pleasing and acceptable to God in Christ, and spring out of a true and lively faith, insomuch that by them a lively faith may be as evidently known as a tree is discerned by its fruit.

Article XI.—Of Works of Supererogation

Voluntary works—besides, over and above God's commandments—which they call works of supererogation, cannot be taught without arrogancy and impiety. For by them men do declare that they do not only render unto God as much as they are bound to do, but that they do more for his sake than of bounden duty is required; whereas Christ saith plainly: When you have done all that is commanded you, say, We are unprofitable servants.

Article XII.—Of Sin After Justification

Not every sin willingly committed after justification is the sin against the Holy Ghost, and unpardonable. Wherefore, the grant of repentance is not to be denied to such as fall into sin after justification. After we have received the Holy Ghost, we may depart from grace given, and fall into sin, and, by the grace of God, rise again and amend our lives. And therefore they are to be condemned who say they can no more sin as long as they live here; or deny the place of forgiveness to such as truly repent.

Article XIII.—Of the Church

The visible Church of Christ is a congregation of faithful men in which the pure Word of God is preached, and the Sacraments duly administered according to Christ's ordinance, in all those things that of necessity are requisite to the same.

Article XIV.—Of Purgatory[5]

The Romish doctrine concerning purgatory, pardon, worshiping, and adoration, as well of images as of relics, and also invocation of saints, is a fond thing, vainly invented, and grounded upon no warrant of Scripture, but repugnant to the Word of God.

Article XV.—Of Speaking in the Congregation in Such a Tongue as the People Understand

It is a thing plainly repugnant to the Word of God, and the custom of the primitive Church, to have public prayer in the church, or to minister the Sacraments, in a tongue not understood by the people.

Article XVI.—Of the Sacraments

Sacraments ordained of Christ are not only badges or tokens of Christian men's profession, but rather they are certain signs of grace, and God's good will toward us, by which he doth work

---

[5]For the contemporary interpretation of this and similar articles (i.e., Articles XIV, XV, XVI, XVIII, XIX, XX and XXI), *see* A Resolution of Intent of the General Conference of 1970 (*Journal*, pp. 254-55) and The Book of Resolutions (1968, pp. 65-72).

invisibly in us, and doth not only quicken, but also strengthen and confirm, our faith in him.

There are two Sacraments ordained of Christ our Lord in the Gospel; that is to say, Baptism and the Supper of the Lord.

Those five commonly called sacraments, that is to say, confirmation, penance, orders, matrimony, and extreme unction, are not to be counted for Sacraments of the Gospel; being such as have partly grown out of the *corrupt* following of the apostles, and partly are states of life allowed in the Scriptures, but yet have not the like nature of Baptism and the Lord's Supper, because they have not any visible sign or ceremony ordained of God.

The Sacraments were not ordained of Christ to be gazed upon, or to be carried about; but that we should duly use them. And in such only as worthily receive the same, they have a wholesome effect or operation; but they that receive them unworthily, purchase to themselves condemnation, as St. Paul saith.

Article XVII.—Of Baptism

Baptism is not only a sign of profession and mark of difference whereby Christians are distinguished from others that are not baptized; but it is also a sign of regeneration or the new birth. The baptism of young children is to be retained in the church.[6]

Article XVIII.—Of the Lord's Supper

The Supper of the Lord is not only a sign of the love that Christians ought to have among themselves one to another, but rather is a sacrament of our redemption by Christ's death; insomuch that, to such as rightly, worthily, and with faith receive the same, the bread which we break is a partaking of the body of Christ; and likewise the cup of blessing is a partaking of the blood of Christ.

---

[6]*See* Judicial Council Decision 142.

Transubstantiation, or the change of the substance of bread and wine in the Supper of our Lord, cannot be proved by Holy Writ, but is repugnant to the plain words of Scripture, overthroweth the nature of a sacrament, and hath given occasion to many superstitions.

The body of Christ is given, taken, and eaten in the Supper, only after a heavenly and spiritual manner. And the mean whereby the body of Christ is received and eaten in the Supper is faith.

The Sacrament of the Lord's Supper was not by Christ's ordinance reserved, carried about, lifted up, or worshiped.

Article XIX.—Of Both Kinds

The cup of the Lord is not to be denied to the lay people; for both the parts of the Lord's Supper, by Christ's ordinance and commandment, ought to be administered to all Christians alike.

Article XX.—Of the One Oblation of Christ, Finished upon the Cross

The offering of Christ, once made, is that perfect redemption, propitiation, and satisfaction for all the sins of the whole world, both original and actual; and there is none other satisfaction for sin but that alone. Wherefore the sacrifice of masses, in the which it is commonly said that the priest doth offer Christ for the quick and the dead, to have remission of pain or guilt, is a blasphemous fable and dangerous deceit.

Article XXI.—Of the Marriage of Ministers

The ministers of Christ are not commanded by God's law either to vow the estate of single life, or to abstain from marriage; therefore it is lawful for them, as for all other Christians, to marry at their own discretion, as they shall judge the same to serve best to godliness.

Article XXII.—Of the Rites and Ceremonies of Churches

It is not necessary that rites and ceremonies should in all places be the same, or exactly alike; for they have been always different, and may be changed according to the diversity of countries, times, and men's manners, so that nothing be ordained against God's Word. Whosoever, through his private judgment, willingly and purposely doth openly break the rites and ceremonies of the church to which he belongs, which are not repugnant to the Word of God, and are ordained and approved by common authority, ought to be rebuked openly, that others may fear to do the like, as one that offendeth against the common order of the church, and woundeth the consciences of weak brethren.

Every particular church may ordain, change, or abolish rites and ceremonies, so that all things may be done to edification.

Article XXIII.—Of the Rulers of the United States of America

The President, the Congress, the general assemblies, the governors, and the councils of state, *as the delegates of the people,* are the rulers of the United States of America, according to the division of power made to them by the Constitution of the United States and by the constitutions of their respective states. And the said states are a sovereign and independent nation, and ought not to be subject to any foreign jurisdiction.

Article XXIV.—Of Christian Men's Goods

The riches and goods of Christians are not common as touching the right, title, and possession of the same, as some do falsely boast. Notwithstanding, every man ought, of such things as he possesseth, liberally to give alms to the poor, according to his ability.

Article XXV.—Of a Christian Man's Oath

As we confess that vain and rash swearing is forbidden Christian men by our Lord Jesus Christ and James his apostle, so we judge that the Christian religion doth not prohibit, but that a man may swear when the magistrate requireth, in a cause of faith and charity, so it be done according to the prophet's teaching, in justice, judgment, and truth.

[The following Article from the Methodist Protestant *Discipline* is placed here by the Uniting Conference (1939). It was not one of the Articles of Religion voted upon by the three churches.]

Of Sanctification

Sanctification is that renewal of our fallen nature by the Holy Ghost, received through faith in Jesus Christ, whose blood of atonement cleanseth from all sin; whereby we are not only delivered from the guilt of sin, but are washed from its pollution, saved from its power, and are enabled, through grace, to love God with all our hearts and to walk in his holy commandments blameless.

[The following provision was adopted by the Uniting Conference (1939). This statement seeks to interpret to our churches in foreign lands Article XXIII of the Articles of Religion. It is a legislative enactment but is not a part of the Constitution. (*See* Judicial Council Decisions 41, 176, and Decision 6, Interim Judicial Council.)]

Of the Duty of Christians to the Civil Authority

It is the duty of all Christians, and especially of all Christian ministers, to observe and obey the laws and commands of the governing or supreme authority of the country of which they are citizens or subjects or in which they reside, and to use all laudable means to encourage and enjoin obedience to the powers that be.

THE CONFESSION OF FAITH
OF THE EVANGELICAL UNITED BRETHREN CHURCH[7]

[Bibliographical Note: The text of the Confession of Faith is identical with that of its original in *The Discipline of The Evangelical United Brethren Church* (1963).]

Article I.—God

We believe in the one true, holy and living God, Eternal Spirit, who is Creator, Sovereign and Preserver of all things

---

[7]Protected by Restrictive Rule 2 (¶ 16).

visible and invisible. He is infinite in power, wisdom, justice, goodness and love, and rules with gracious regard for the well-being and salvation of men, to the glory of his name. We believe the one God reveals himself as the Trinity: Father, Son and Holy Spirit, distinct but inseparable, eternally one in essence and power.

Article II.—Jesus Christ

We believe in Jesus Christ, truly God and truly man, in whom the divine and human natures are perfectly and inseparably united. He is the eternal Word made flesh, the only begotten Son of the Father, born of the Virgin Mary by the power of the Holy Spirit. As ministering Servant he lived, suffered and died on the cross. He was buried, rose from the dead and ascended into heaven to be with the Father, from whence he shall return. He is eternal Savior and Mediator, who intercedes for us, and by him all men will be judged.

Article III.—The Holy Spirit

We believe in the Holy Spirit who proceeds from and is one in being with the Father and the Son. He convinces the world of sin, of righteousness and of judgment. He leads men through faithful response to the gospel into the fellowship of the Church. He comforts, sustains and empowers the faithful and guides them into all truth.

Article IV.—The Holy Bible

We believe the Holy Bible, Old and New Testaments, reveals the Word of God so far as it is necessary for our salvation. It is to be received through the Holy Spirit as the true rule and guide for faith and practice. Whatever is not revealed in or established by the Holy Scriptures is not to be made an article of faith nor is it to be taught as essential to salvation.

Article V.—The Church

We believe the Christian Church is the community of all true believers under the Lordship of Christ. We believe it is one, holy, apostolic and catholic. It is the redemptive fellowship in which the Word of God is preached by men divinely called, and the sacraments are duly administered according to Christ's own appointment. Under the discipline of the Holy Spirit the Church exists for the maintenance of worship, the edification of believers and the redemption of the world.

Article VI.—The Sacraments

We believe the sacraments, ordained by Christ, are symbols and pledges of the Christian's profession and of God's love toward us. They are means of grace by which God works invisibly in us, quickening, strengthening and confirming our faith in him. Two sacraments are ordained by Christ our Lord, namely Baptism and the Lord's Supper.

We believe Baptism signifies entrance into the household of faith, and is a symbol of repentance and inner cleansing from sin, a representation of the new birth in Christ Jesus and a mark of Christian discipleship.

We believe children are under the atonement of Christ and as heirs of the Kingdom of God are acceptable subjects for Christian baptism. Children of believing parents through baptism become the special responsibility of the Church. They should be nurtured and led to personal acceptance of Christ, and by profession of faith confirm their baptism.

We believe the Lord's Supper is a representation of our redemption, a memorial of the sufferings and death of Christ, and a token of love and union which Christians have with Christ and with one another. Those who rightly, worthily and in faith eat the broken bread and drink the blessed cup partake of the body and blood of Christ in a spiritual manner until he comes.

Article VII.—Sin and Free Will

We believe man is fallen from righteousness and, apart from the grace of our Lord Jesus Christ, is destitute of holiness and inclined to evil. Except a man be born again, he cannot see the Kingdom of God. In his own strength, without divine grace, man cannot do good works pleasing and acceptable to God. We believe, however, man influenced and empowered by the Holy Spirit is responsible in freedom to exercise his will for good.

Article VIII.—Reconciliation Through Christ

We believe God was in Christ reconciling the world to himself. The offering Christ freely made on the cross is the perfect and sufficient sacrifice for the sins of the whole world, redeeming man from all sin, so that no other satisfaction is required.

Article IX.—Justification and Regeneration

We believe we are never accounted righteous before God through our works or merit, but that penitent sinners are justified or accounted righteous before God only by faith in our Lord Jesus Christ.

We believe regeneration is the renewal of man in righteousness through Jesus Christ, by the power of the Holy Spirit, whereby we are made partakers of the divine nature and experience newness of life. By this new birth the believer becomes reconciled to God and is enabled to serve him with the will and the affections.

We believe, although we have experienced regeneration, it is possible to depart from grace and fall into sin; and we may even then, by the grace of God, be renewed in righteousness.

Article X.—Good Works

We believe good works are the necessary fruits of faith and follow regeneration but they do not have the virtue to remove our sins or to avert divine judgment. We believe good works, pleasing and acceptable to God in Christ, spring from a true and living faith, for through and by them faith is made evident. —

Article XI.—Sanctification and Christian Perfection

We believe sanctification is the work of God's grace through the Word and the Spirit, by which those who have been born again are cleansed from sin in their thoughts, words and acts, and are enabled to live in accordance with God's will, and to strive for holiness without which no one will see the Lord.

Entire sanctification is a state of perfect love, righteousness and true holiness which every regenerate believer may obtain by being delivered from the power of sin, by loving God with all the heart, soul, mind and strength, and by loving one's neighbor as one's self. Through faith in Jesus Christ this gracious gift may be received in this life both gradually and instantaneously, and should be sought earnestly by every child of God.

We believe this experience does not deliver us from the infirmities, ignorance, and mistakes common to man, nor from the possibilities of further sin. The Christian must continue on guard against spiritual pride and seek to gain victory over every temptation to sin. He must respond wholly to the will of God so that sin will lose its power over him; and the world, the flesh, and the devil are put under his feet. Thus he rules over these enemies with watchfulness through the power of the Holy Spirit.

Article XII.—The Judgment and the Future State

We believe all men stand under the righteous judgment of Jesus Christ, both now and in the last day. We believe in the resurrection of the dead; the righteous to life eternal and the wicked to endless condemnation.

Article XIII.—Public Worship

We believe divine worship is the duty and privilege of man who, in the presence of God, bows in adoration, humility and dedication. We believe divine worship is essential to the life of the Church, and that the assembling of the people of God for such worship is necessary to Christian fellowship and spiritual growth.

We believe the order of public worship need not be the same in all places but may be modified by the Church according to circumstances and the needs of men. It should be in a language and form understood by the people, consistent with the Holy Scriptures to the edification of all, and in accordance with the order and *Discipline* of the Church.

Article XIV.—The Lord's Day

We believe the Lord's Day is divinely ordained for private and public worship, for rest from unnecessary work, and should be devoted to spiritual improvement, Christian fellowship and service. It is commemorative of our Lord's resurrection and is an emblem of our eternal rest. It is essential to the permanence and growth of the Christian Church, and important to the welfare of the civil community.

Article XV.—The Christian and Property

We believe God is the owner of all things and that the individual holding of property is lawful and is a sacred trust under God. Private property is to be used for the manifestation of Christian love and liberality, and to support the Church's mission in the world. All forms of property, whether private, corporate or public, are to be held in solemn trust and used responsibly for human good under the sovereignty of God.

Article XVI.—Civil Government

We believe civil government derives its just powers from the sovereign God. As Christians we recognize the governments under whose protection we reside and believe such governments should be based on, and be responsible for, the recognition of human rights under God. We believe war and bloodshed are contrary to the gospel and spirit of Christ. We believe it is the duty of Christian citizens to give moral strength and purpose to their respective governments through sober, righteous and godly living.

THE STANDARD SERMONS OF WESLEY

[Bibliographical Note: The Wesleyan "standards" have been reprinted frequently. The critical edition of Wesley's *Sermons* is included in *The Works of John Wesley,* vols. 1–4 (Nashville: Abingdon Press, 1984-87).]

THE EXPLANATORY NOTES UPON THE NEW TESTAMENT

[Bibliographical Note: *The Explanatory Notes Upon the New Testament* (1755) is currently in print (Ward's 1976 edition) and is forthcoming as vols. 5–6 of *The Works of John Wesley.*]

THE GENERAL RULES OF THE METHODIST CHURCH[8]

[Bibliographical Note: The General Rules are printed here in the text of 1808 (when the fifth Restrictive Rule took effect), as subsequently amended by constitutional actions in 1848 and 1868.]

The Nature, Design, and General Rules of Our United Societies

In the latter end of the year 1739 eight or ten persons came to Mr. Wesley, in London, who appeared to be deeply convinced of sin, and earnestly groaning for redemption. They desired, as did two or three more the next day, that he would spend some time with them in prayer, and advise them how to flee from the wrath to come, which they saw continually hanging over their heads. That he might have more time for this great work, he appointed a day when they might all come together, which from thenceforward they did every week, namely, on Thursday in the evening. To these, and as many more as desired to join with them (for their number increased daily), he gave those advices from time to time which he judged most needful for them, and they

---

[8]Protected by Restrictive Rule 5 (¶ 19).

always concluded their meeting with prayer suited to their several necessities.

This was the rise of the **United Society,** first in Europe, and then in America. Such a society is no other than "a company of men having the *form* and seeking the *power* of godliness, united in order to pray together, to receive the word of exhortation, and to watch over one another in love, that they may help each other to work out their salvation."

That it may the more easily be discerned whether they are indeed working out their own salvation, each society is divided into smaller companies, called **classes,** according to their respective places of abode. There are about twelve persons in a class, one of whom is styled the **leader.** It is his duty:

1. To see each person in his class once a week at least, in order: (1) to inquire how their souls prosper; (2) to advise, reprove, comfort or exhort, as occasion may require; (3) to receive what they are willing to give toward the relief of the preachers, church, and poor.

2. To meet the ministers and the stewards of the society once a week, in order: (1) to inform the minister of any that are sick, or of any that walk disorderly and will not be reproved; (2) to pay the stewards what they have received of their several classes in the week preceding.

There is only one condition previously required of those who desire admission into these societies: "a desire to flee from the wrath to come, and to be saved from their sins." But wherever this is really fixed in the soul it will be shown by its fruits.

It is therefore expected of all who continue therein that they should continue to evidence their desire of salvation,

First: By doing no harm, by avoiding evil of every kind, especially that which is most generally practiced, such as:

The taking of the name of God in vain.

The profaning the day of the Lord, either by doing ordinary work therein or by buying or selling.

Drunkenness: buying or selling spirituous liquors, or drinking them, unless in cases of extreme necessity.

Slaveholding; buying or selling slaves.

Fighting, quarreling, brawling, brother going to law with brother; returning evil for evil, or railing for railing; the using many words in buying or selling.

The buying or selling goods that have not paid the duty.

The giving or taking things on usury—i.e., unlawful interest.

Uncharitable or unprofitable conversation; particularly speaking evil of magistrates or of ministers.

Doing to others as we would not they should do unto us.

Doing what we know is not for the glory of God, as:

The putting on of gold and costly apparel.

The taking such diversions as cannot be used in the name of the Lord Jesus.

The singing those songs, or reading those books, which do not tend to the knowledge or love of God.

Softness and needless self-indulgence.

Laying up treasure upon earth.

Borrowing without a probability of paying; or taking up goods without a probability of paying for them.

It is expected of all who continue in these societies that they should continue to evidence their desire of salvation,

Secondly: By doing good; by being in every kind merciful after their power; as they have opportunity, doing good of every possible sort, and, as far as possible, to all men:

To their bodies, of the ability which God giveth, by giving food to the hungry, by clothing the naked, by visiting or helping them that are sick or in prison.

To their souls, by instructing, reproving, or exhorting all we have any intercourse with; trampling under foot that enthusiastic doctrine that "we are not to do good unless *our hearts be free to it."*

By doing good, especially to them that are of the household of faith or groaning so to be; employing them preferably to others; buying one of another, helping each other in business, and so much the more because the world will love its own and them only.

By all possible diligence and frugality, that the gospel be not blamed.

By running with patience the race which is set before them, denying themselves, and taking up their cross daily; submitting to bear the reproach of Christ, to be as the filth and offscouring of the world; and looking that men should say all manner of evil of them *falsely,* for the Lord's sake.

It is expected of all who desire to continue in these societies that they should continue to evidence their desire of salvation, *Thirdly:* By attending upon all the ordinances of God; such are:

The public worship of God.
The ministry of the Word, either read or expounded.
The Supper of the Lord.
Family and private prayer.
Searching the Scriptures.
Fasting or abstinence.

These are the General Rules of our societies; all of which we are taught of God to observe, even in his written Word, which is the only rule, and the sufficient rule, both of our faith and practice. And all these we know his Spirit writes on truly awakened hearts. If there be any among us who observe them not, who habitually break any of them, let it be known unto them who watch over that soul as they who must give an account. We will admonish him of the error of his ways. We will bear with him for a season. But then, if he repent not, he hath no more place among us. We have delivered our own souls.

¶ 69. SECTION 4—OUR THEOLOGICAL TASK

Theology is our effort to reflect upon God's gracious action in our lives. In response to the love of Christ, we desire to be drawn into a deeper relationship with the "author and perfecter of our faith." Our theological explorations seek to give expression to the mysterious reality of God's presence, peace, and power in the world. By so doing, we attempt to articulate more clearly our understanding of the divine–human encounter and are thereby more fully prepared to participate in God's work in the world.

The theological task, though related to the Church's doctrinal expressions, serves a different function. Our doctrinal affirmations assist us in the discernment of Christian truth in ever-changing contexts. Our theological task includes the testing, renewal, elaboration, and application of our doctrinal perspective in carrying out our calling "to spread scriptural holiness over these lands."

While the Church considers its doctrinal affirmations a central feature of its identity and restricts official changes to a constitutional process, the Church encourages serious reflection across the theological spectrum.

As United Methodists, we are called to identify the needs both of individuals and of society and to address those needs out of the resources of Christian faith in a way that is clear, convincing, and effective. Theology serves the Church by interpreting the world's needs and challenges to the Church and by interpreting the gospel to the world.

The Nature of Our Theological Task

Our theological task is both critical and constructive. It is *critical* in that we test various expressions of faith by asking, Are they true? Appropriate? Clear? Cogent? Credible? Are they based on love? Do they provide the Church and its members with a witness that is faithful to the gospel as reflected in our living heritage and that is authentic and convincing in the light of human experience and the present state of human knowledge?

Our theological task is *constructive* in that every generation must appropriate creatively the wisdom of the past and seek God in their midst in order to think afresh about God, revelation, sin, redemption, worship, the Church, freedom, justice, moral responsibility, and other significant theological concerns. Our summons is to understand and receive the gospel promises in our troubled and uncertain times.

Our theological task is both individual and communal. It is a feature in the ministry of *individual* Christians. It requires the participation of all who are in our Church, lay and ordained, because the mission of the Church is to be carried out by everyone who is called to discipleship. To be persons of faith is to hunger to understand the truth given to us in Jesus Christ.

Theological inquiry is by no means a casual undertaking. It requires sustained disciplines of study, reflection, and prayer.

Yet the discernment of "plain truth for plain people" is not limited to theological specialists. Scholars have their role to play in assisting the people of God to fulfill this calling, but all Christians are called to theological reflection.

Our theological task is *communal*. It unfolds in conversations open to the experiences, insights, and traditions of all constituencies that make up United Methodism.

This dialogue belongs to the life of every congregation. It is fostered by laity and clergy, by the bishops, by the boards, agencies, and theological schools of the Church.

Conferences speak and act for United Methodists in their official decisions at appropriate levels. Our conciliar and representative forms of decision-making do not release United Methodists as individuals from the responsibility to develop sound theological judgment.

Our theological task is contextual and incarnational. It is grounded upon God's supreme mode of self-revelation—the incarnation in Jesus Christ. God's eternal Word comes to us in flesh and blood in a given time and place, and in full identification with humanity. Therefore, theological reflection is energized by our incarnational involvement in the daily life of the Church and the world, as we participate in God's liberating and saving action.

Our theological task is essentially practical. It informs the individual's daily decisions and serves the Church's life and work. While highly theoretical constructions of Christian thought make important contributions to theological understanding, we finally measure the truth of such statements in relation to their practical significance. Our interest is to incorporate the promises and demands of the gospel into our daily lives.

Theological inquiry can clarify our thinking about what we are to say and do. It presses us to pay attention to the world around us.

Realities of intense human suffering, threats to the survival of life, and challenges to human dignity confront us afresh with fundamental theological issues: the nature and purposes of God, the relations of human beings to one another, the nature of human freedom and responsibility, and the care and proper use of all creation.

Theological Guidelines: Sources and Criteria

As United Methodists, we have an obligation to bear a faithful Christian witness to Jesus Christ, the living reality at the center of the Church's life and witness. To fulfill this obligation, we reflect critically on our biblical and theological inheritance, striving to express faithfully the witness we make in our own time.

Two considerations are central to this endeavor: the sources from which we derive our theological affirmations and the criteria by which we assess the adequacy of our understanding and witness.

Wesley believed that the living core of the Christian faith was revealed in Scripture, illumined by tradition, vivified in personal experience, and confirmed by reason.

Scripture is primary, revealing the Word of God "so far as it is necessary for our salvation." Therefore, our theological task, in both its critical and constructive aspects, focuses on disciplined study of the Bible.

To aid his study of the Bible and deepen his understanding of faith, Wesley drew on Christian tradition, in particular the Patristic writings, the ecumenical creeds, the teachings of the Reformers, and the literature of contemporary spirituality.

Thus, tradition provides both a source and a measure of authentic Christian witness, though its authority derives from its faithfulness to the biblical message.

The Christian witness, even when grounded in Scripture and mediated by tradition, is ineffectual unless understood and appropriated by the individual. To become our witness, it must make sense in terms of our own reason and experience.

For Wesley, a cogent account of the Christian faith required the use of reason, both to understand Scripture and to relate the biblical message to wider fields of knowledge. He looked for confirmations of the biblical witness in human experience, especially the experiences of regeneration and sanctification, but also in the "common sense" knowledge of everyday experience.

The interaction of these sources and criteria in Wesley's own theology furnishes a guide for our continuing theological task as United Methodists. In that task Scripture, as the constitutive witness to the wellsprings of our faith, occupies a place of primary authority among these theological sources.

In practice, theological reflection may also find its point of departure in tradition, experience, or rational analysis. What matters most is that all four guidelines be brought to bear in faithful, serious, theological consideration. Insights arising from serious study of the Scriptures and tradition enrich contemporary experience. Imaginative and critical thought enables us to understand better the Bible and our common Christian history.

Scripture

United Methodists share with other Christians the conviction that Scripture is the primary source and criterion for Christian doctrine. Through Scripture the living Christ meets us in the experience of redeeming grace. We are convinced that Jesus Christ is the living Word of God in our midst whom we trust in life and death.

The biblical authors, illumined by the Holy Spirit, bear witness that in Christ the world is reconciled to God. The Bible bears authentic testimony to God's self-disclosure in the life, death, and resurrection of Jesus Christ as well as in God's work of creation, in the pilgrimage of Israel, and in the Holy Spirit's ongoing activity in human history.

As we open our minds and hearts to the Word of God through the words of human beings inspired by the Holy Spirit, faith is born and nourished, our understanding is deepened, and the possibilities for transforming the world become apparent to us.

The Bible is sacred canon for Christian people, formally acknowledged as such by historic ecumenical councils of the Church. Our doctrinal standards identify as canonical thirty-nine books of the Old Testament and the twenty-seven books of the New Testament.

Our standards affirm the Bible as the source of all that is "necessary" and "sufficient" unto salvation (Articles of Religion) and "is to be received through the Holy Spirit as the true rule and guide for faith and practice" (Confession of Faith).

We properly read Scripture within the believing community, informed by the tradition of that community. We interpret individual texts in light of their place in the Bible as a whole.

We are aided by scholarly inquiry and personal insight, under the guidance of the Holy Spirit. As we work with each text, we take into account what we have been able to learn about the original context and intention of that text. In this understanding we draw upon the careful historical, literary, and textual studies of recent years, which have enriched our understanding of the Bible.

Through this faithful reading of Scripture, we may come to know the truth of the biblical message in its bearing on our own lives and the life of the world. Thus the Bible serves both as a source of our faith and as the basic criterion by which the truth and fidelity of any interpretation of faith is measured.

While we acknowledge the primacy of Scripture in theological reflection, our attempts to grasp its meaning always involve tradition, experience, and reason. Like Scripture, these may become creative vehicles of the Holy Spirit as they function within the Church. They quicken our faith, open our eyes to the wonder of God's love, and clarify our understanding.

The Wesleyan heritage, reflecting its origins in the catholic and reformed ethos of English Christianity, directs us to a self-conscious use of these three sources in interpreting Scripture and in formulating faith statements based on the biblical witness. These sources are, along with Scripture, indispensable to our theological task.

The close relationship of tradition, experience, and reason appears in the Bible itself. Scripture witnesses to a variety of diverse traditions, some of which reflect tensions in interpretation within the early Judeo-Christian heritage. However, these traditions are woven together in the Bible in a manner that expresses the fundamental unity of God's revelation as received and experienced by people in the diversity of their own lives.

The developing communities of faith judged them, therefore, to be an authoritative witness to that revelation. In recognizing the interrelationship and inseparability of the four basic resources for theological understanding, we are following a model which is present in the biblical text itself.

Tradition

The theological task does not start anew in each age or each person. Christianity does not leap from New Testament times to the present as though nothing were to be learned from that great cloud of witnesses in between. For centuries Christians have sought to interpret the truth of the gospel for their time.

In these attempts, tradition, understood both in terms of process and form, has played an important role. The passing on and receiving of the gospel among persons, regions, and generations constitutes a dynamic element of Christian history. The formulations and practices that grew out of specific circumstances constitute the legacy of the corporate experience of earlier Christian communities.

These traditions are found in many cultures around the globe. But the history of Christianity includes a mixture of ignorance, misguided zeal, and sin. Scripture remains the norm by which all traditions are judged.

The story of the Church reflects the most basic sense of tradition, the continuing activity of God's Spirit transforming human life. Tradition is the history of that continuing environment of grace in and by which all Christians live, God's self-giving love in Jesus Christ. As such, tradition transcends the story of particular traditions.

In this deeper sense of tradition, all Christians share a common history. Within that history, Christian tradition precedes Scripture, and yet Scripture comes to be the focal expression of the tradition. As United Methodists, we pursue our theological task in openness to the richness of both the form and power of tradition.

The multiplicity of traditions furnishes a richly varied source for theological reflection and construction. For United Methodists, certain strands of tradition have special importance as the historic foundation of our doctrinal heritage and the distinctive expressions of our communal existence.

We are now challenged by traditions from around the world which accent dimensions of Christian understanding that grow out of the sufferings and victories of the downtrodden. These traditions help us rediscover the biblical witness to God's special commitment to the poor, the disabled, the imprisoned, the oppressed, the outcast. In these persons we encounter the living presence of Jesus Christ.

These traditions underscore the equality of all persons in Jesus Christ. They display the capacity of the gospel to free us to embrace the diversity of human cultures and appreciate their values. They reinforce our traditional understanding of the inseparability of personal salvation and social justice. They deepen our commitment to global peace.

A critical appreciation of these traditions can compel us to think about God in new ways, enlarge our vision of shalom, and enhance our confidence in God's provident love.

Tradition acts as a measure of validity and propriety for a community's faith insofar as it represents a consensus of faith. The various traditions that presently make claims upon us may contain conflicting images and insights of truth and validity. We examine such conflicts in light of Scripture, reflecting critically upon the doctrinal stance of our Church.

It is by the discerning use of our standards and in openness to emerging forms of Christian identity that we attempt to maintain fidelity to the apostolic faith.

At the same time, we continue to draw on the broader Christian tradition as an expression of the history of divine grace within which Christians are able to recognize and welcome one another in love.

Experience

In our theological task, we follow Wesley's practice of examining experience, both individual and corporate, for confirmations of the realities of God's grace attested in Scripture.

Our experience interacts with Scripture. We read Scripture in light of the conditions and events that help shape who we are, and we interpret our experience in terms of Scripture.

All religious experience affects all human experience; all human experience affects our understanding of religious experience.

On the personal level, experience is to the individual as tradition is to the Church: it is the personal appropriation of God's forgiving and empowering grace. Experience authenticates in our own lives the truths revealed in Scripture and illumined in tradition, enabling us to claim the Christian witness as our own.

Wesley described faith and its assurance as "a sure trust and confidence" in the mercy of God through our Lord Jesus Christ, and a steadfast hope of all good things to be received at God's hand. Such assurance is God's gracious gift through the witness of the Holy Spirit.

This "new life in Christ" is what we as United Methodists mean when we speak of "Christian experience." Christian experience gives us new eyes to see the living truth in Scripture. It confirms the biblical message for our present. It illumines our understanding of God and creation, and motivates us to make sensitive moral judgments.

Although profoundly personal, Christian experience is also corporate; our theological task is informed by the experience of the Church and by the common experiences of all humanity. In our attempts to understand the biblical message, we recognize that God's gift of liberating love embraces the whole of creation.

Some facets of human experience tax our theological understanding. Many of God's people live in terror, hunger, loneliness, and degradation. Everyday experiences of birth and death, of growth and life in the created world, and an awareness of wider social relations also belong to serious theological reflection.

A new awareness of such experiences can inform our appropriation of scriptural truths and sharpen our appreciation of the good news of the Kingdom of God.

As a source for theological reflection, experience, like tradition, is richly varied, challenging our efforts to put into words the totality of the promises of the gospel. We interpret experience in the light of scriptural norms, just as our experience informs our reading of the biblical message. In this respect,

Scripture remains central in our efforts to be faithful in making our Christian witness.

Reason

Although we recognize that God's revelation and our experiences of God's grace continually surpass the scope of human language and reason, we also believe that any disciplined theological work calls for the careful use of reason.

By reason we read and interpret Scripture.

By reason we determine whether our Christian witness is clear.

By reason we ask questions of faith and seek to understand God's action and will.

By reason we organize the understandings that compose our witness and render them internally coherent.

By reason we test the congruence of our witness to the biblical testimony and to the traditions which mediate that testimony to us.

By reason we relate our witness to the full range of human knowledge, experience, and service.

Since all truth is from God, efforts to discern the connections between revelation and reason, faith and science, grace and nature, are useful endeavors in developing credible and communicable doctrine. We seek nothing less than a total view of reality that is decisively informed by the promises and imperatives of the Christian gospel, though we know well that such an attempt will always be marred by the limits and distortions characteristic of human knowledge.

Nevertheless, by our quest for reasoned understandings of Christian faith we seek to grasp, express, and live out the gospel in a way that will commend itself to thoughtful persons who are seeking to know and follow God's ways.

In theological reflection, the resources of tradition, experience, and reason are integral to our study of Scripture without displacing Scripture's primacy for faith and practice. These four sources—each making distinctive contributions, yet all finally working together—guide our quest as United Methodists for a vital and appropriate Christian witness.

The Present Challenge to Theology in the Church

In addition to historic tensions and conflicts that still require resolution, new issues continually arise that summon us to fresh theological inquiry. Daily we are presented with an array of concerns that challenge our proclamation of God's reign over all of human existence.

Of crucial importance are concerns generated by great human struggles for dignity, liberation, and fulfillment—aspirations that are inherent elements in God's design for creation. These concerns are borne by theologies that express the heart cries of the downtrodden and the aroused indignation of the compassionate.

The perils of nuclear destruction, terrorism, war, poverty, violence, and injustice confront us. Injustices linked to race, gender, class, and age are widespread in our times. Misuse of natural resources and disregard for the fragile balances in our environment contradict our calling to care for God's creation. Secularism pervades high-technology civilizations, hindering human awareness of the spiritual depths of existence.

We seek an authentic Christian response to these realities, that the healing and redeeming work of God might be present in our words and deeds. Too often, theology is used to support practices that are unjust. We look for answers that are in harmony with the gospel and do not claim exemption from critical assessment.

A rich quality of our Church, especially as it has developed in the last century, is its global character. We are a church with a distinctive theological heritage, but that heritage is lived out in a global community, resulting in understandings of our faith enriched by indigenous experiences and manners of expression.

We affirm the contributions which United Methodists of varying ethnic, language, cultural, and national groups make to one another and to our Church as a whole. We celebrate our shared commitment to clear theological understanding and vital missional expression.

United Methodists as a diverse people continue to strive for consensus in understanding the gospel. In our diversity, we are held together by a shared inheritance and a common desire to participate in the creative and redemptive activity of God.

Our task is to articulate our vision in a way that will draw us together as a people in mission.

In the name of Jesus Christ we are called to work within our diversity while exercising patience and forbearance with one another. Such patience stems neither from indifference toward truth nor from an indulgent tolerance of error but from an awareness that we know only in part and that none of us is able to search the mysteries of God except by the Spirit of God. We proceed with our theological task, trusting that the Spirit will grant us wisdom to continue our journey with the whole people of God.

Ecumenical Commitment

Christian unity is founded on the theological understanding that in our Baptism, we are made members-in-common of the one Body of Christ. Christian unity is not an option; it is a gift to be received and expressed.

United Methodists respond to the theological, biblical, and practical mandates for Christian unity by firmly committing ourselves to the cause of Christian unity at local, national, and world levels. We invest ourselves in many ways by which mutual recognition of churches, of members, and of ministries may lead us to sharing in Holy Communion with all of God's people.

Knowing that denominational loyalty is always subsumed in our life in the Church of Jesus Christ, we welcome and celebrate the rich experience of United Methodist leadership in church councils and consultations, in multilateral and bilateral dialogues, as well as in other forms of ecumenical convergence that have led to the healing of churches and nations.

We see the Holy Spirit at work in making the unity among us more visible.

Concurrently, we have entered into serious interfaith encounters and explorations between Christians and adherents of other living faiths of the world. Scripture calls us to be both neighbors and witnesses to all peoples. Such encounters require us to reflect anew on our faith and seek guidance for our witness among neighbors of other faiths. We then rediscover that the God who has acted in Jesus Christ for the salvation of the whole world is also the Creator of all humankind, the One who is "above all and through all and in all" (Ephesians 4:6).

As people bound together on one planet, we see the need for a self-critical view of our own tradition and accurate appreciation of other traditions. In these encounters, our aim is not to reduce doctrinal differences to some lowest common denominator of religious agreement but to raise all such relationships to the highest possible level of human fellowship and understanding.

We labor together with the help of God toward the salvation, health, and peace of all people. In respectful conversations and in practical cooperation, we confess our Christian faith and strive to display the manner in which Jesus Christ is the life and hope of the world.

Conclusion

Doctrine arises out of the life of the Church—its faith, its worship, its discipline, its conflicts, its challenges from the world it would serve.

Evangelism, nurture, and mission require a constant effort to integrate authentic experience, rational thought, and purposeful action with theological integrity.

A convincing witness to our Lord and Savior Jesus Christ can contribute to the renewal of our faith, bring persons to that faith, and strengthen the Church as an agent of healing and reconciliation.

This witness, however, cannot fully describe or encompass the mystery of God. Though we experience the wonder of God's grace at work with us and among us, and though we know the joy of the present signs of God's kingdom, each new step makes us more aware of the ultimate mystery of God, from which arises a heart of wonder and an attitude of humility. Yet we trust that we can know more fully what is essential for our participation in God's saving work in the world, and we are confident in the ultimate unfolding of God's justice and mercy.

In this spirit we take up our theological task, endeavoring to understand the love of God given in Jesus Christ and to spread this love abroad. As we see more clearly who we have been, as we understand more fully the needs of the world, as we draw more effectively upon our theological heritage, we will become better equipped to fulfill our calling as the people of God.

> Now to God
> who by the power at work within us
> is able to do far more abundantly
> than all that we ask or think,
> to God be glory in the church
> and in Christ Jesus to all generations,
> for ever and ever. Amen.
> —Ephesians 3:20-21 (based on RSV)

Glossary

Prepared by Richard P. Heitzenrater

Anabaptists. The name (meaning "rebaptizers") given to various sixteenth-century Protestants who were considered "radical" by the mainline Lutheran and Calvinist reformers because they rejected infant baptism in favor of believer's baptism, usually by immersion.

Apostolic witness of faith. The central affirmations of Christianity as developed within the early Christian community of faith, understood by them to have been transmitted from the disciples of Jesus Christ, contained in those documents that they incorporated into the New Testament, and summarized in such formulations as the Apostles' Creed.

Arianism. The main heresy in the patristic era; denied the full divinity of Jesus Christ; named for its principal proponent, Arius, and deemed heretical at the Council of Nicaea in A.D. 325.

Articles of Religion. The series of doctrinal formulations adopted by the Church of England during the Reformation, eventuating in the Thirty-Nine Articles (1563) that have provided a continuing definition of the Anglican position on the central matters of faith. These were abridged for the American Methodists by John Wesley in 1784 and adopted (with one addition) by The Methodist Episcopal Church as the twenty-five Articles of Religion (see *The Book of Discipline, 1988,* ¶¶ 16, 68).

Assurance. In Wesleyan terms, the witness of the Holy Spirit to believers that they are children of God (justified); experienced by John Wesley at Aldersgate in 1738, who at first required it of all true Christians, then modified his teaching, although still affirming it as a real possibility and normal expectation for all Christians.

Atonement. The reconciliation of God and humanity through the death and resurrection of Jesus Christ (see Articles of Religion, XX; Confession of Faith, VIII).

Augsburg Confession. The Lutheran confession of faith that became an authoritative definition of Lutheran doctrine; adopted first at Augsburg in 1530.

Baptism. The sacramental act whereby a person is cleansed by the Holy Spirit and becomes a part of the body of Christ (see Articles of Religion, XVII; Confession of Faith, VI).

Book of Common Prayer. The official service book of the Church of England since the midsixteenth century, containing the services of Morning and Evening Prayer, the Psalter, forms for administering the sacraments, other rites of the church, and the Articles of Religion.

Calvinism. The system of Reformed doctrine and theology derived from John Calvin and his followers during the sixteenth century (later exhibited in Great Britain and America through Presbyterianism, Puritanism, and the Calvinistic Methodism of George Whitefield). Its main doctrine, the sovereignty of God, resulted in the denial of human free will and the assertion of predestination, which Wesleyan Methodists opposed.

Canon. A term (*kanon* means "reed" or "ruler") used to identify rules or official lists; in Christianity, the term refers on one hand to the list of writings (canonical books) that the church came to regard as comprising Holy Scripture, and on the other hand to a body of ecclesiastical law (canon law) that was distinct from civil law (in this sense used by Asbury to refer to the *Discipline*).

Catholic spirit. Term used by Wesley to denote an approach to religion that stressed unity in the essentials of the Christian faith and toleration in the nonessential forms and modes of religion.

Christian perfection. Wesleyan term for entire sanctification, identified as the fullness of pure love (of God and neighbor), freedom from conscious voluntary sin; a gift of God's grace through the Holy Spirit but not a permanent state of perseverance (see Confession of Faith, XI).

Church. The fellowship of believers in which the pure Word of God is proclaimed and the sacraments duly administered (see Articles of Religion, XIII; Confession of Faith, V); often misconstrued simply as an ecclesiastical organization.

Clergy. Members of the church who have received ordination to the ministry of Word, Sacrament, and Order.

Conciliar. A form of church governance by representative councils with authority, under their leaders, to determine doctrine and discipline; exercised in United Methodism through the various levels of conferences.

Conference. The principal form of governing structure within The United Methodist Church, in the charge, district, annual, jurisdictional, and General Conference; deriving from Wesley's conferences ("conversations") with his preachers and developed in America into a legislative body with lay and clergy participation at every level (compare *conciliar*).

Confession of Faith (1962). Contains the doctrinal standards of the former Evangelical United Brethren Church, being a combination and revision of the doctrinal standards of the two denominations that joined in 1946, the Articles of Religion of The Evangelical Church and the Confession of Faith of The United Brethren Church (see *Discipline*, ¶ 68).

Confessionalism. An approach to orthodoxy or correct doctrine in which a religious group specifies certain formulations of belief (creeds, confessions) to which members are required to assent and by which correct teachings are determined.

Connectionalism. The principle, basic to The United Methodist Church, that all leaders and congregations are connected in a network of loyalties and commitments that support yet supersede local concerns.

Constitution. The document (see *Discipline*, ¶¶ 1–64) that specifies the framework for the structure and operation of The United Methodist Church; adopted at the Uniting Conference (1968), provides the basis for Judicial Council decisions.

Conversion. The change of heart and life in a believer that accompanies faith, bringing divine forgiveness of sins, assurance of God's grace, and the spiritual power to live a new life of love; a concept that combines in various ways some of Wesley's more specific teachings (for example, on repentance, faith, grace, justification, assurance, regeneration, sanctification).

Creeds. Statements of belief (*credo* means "I believe") that present summaries of basic Christian teachings. Some familiar creeds were formulated during the early centuries of the church (for example, the Apostles' Creed, Nicene Creed, Definition of Chalcedon), a few of which continue to be used liturgically and some of which are used by religious bodies as measures of correct doctrine (see *confessionalism*).

Discipline, The Book of Discipline. The collection of regulations that govern the discipline and doctrine (that is, basic structure, operation, and teachings) of The United Methodist Church at all levels; revised by the General Conference every four years.

Doctrinal standards. Documents that contain the officially established teachings of the church, which in turn provide the model by which additional doctrinal statements can be constructed and which furnish a measure by which correct or incorrect teachings can be determined (see *Discipline*, ¶ 68).

Doctrine. An affirmation (*doctrina* means "teaching") by and for the church on matters of faith, approved in some official manner and accepted as an authoritative expression of truth within the particular tradition (compare *theology*).

Ecumenical movement. The movement in the church toward the unity of all Christians (*oikoumene* means "the whole inhabited world"), involving discussions and mutual activities between and among various denominations. The United Methodist Church has a long-standing commitment to and participation in a variety of ecumenical endeavors and organizations.

Experience. A term that can be used to designate personal and corporate appropriations of God's grace (religious encounters such as the witness of the Spirit) or the more general human involvement in the developments of daily life. As a guideline for theological reflection, Wesley most often used the concept in the former sense.

General Conference. The representative body of clergy and laity that meets every four years (quadrennium) to enact legislation and resolutions that will govern The United Methodist Church and speak on its behalf.

General Rules (Nature, Design, and General Rules of the United Societies, 1743). A formulation of three rules that embody the practical implications of Wesley's view of the "way of salvation," representing the vital connection between doctrine and discipline; protected from change by the Fifth Restrictive Rule (see *Discipline*, ¶¶ 19, 66, 68).

Good works. A person's faith working through love—love of God exemplified by works of piety (devotion) and love of neighbor manifested in works of mercy, both made possible by God's grace (see Articles of Religion, X; Confession of Faith, X).

Grace. God's loving mercy and assistance at work in all creation and history through the work of Christ by the Holy Spirit; precedes any human action, available to all, undeserved by any, and fully sufficient for salvation (see Articles of Religion, XVI).

Guidelines, theological. The four basic sources and criteria by which the theological task proceeds—Scripture, tradition, reason, experience; derived from Wesley's understanding of the basic resources and authorities for developing and determining theological and ecclesiastical decisions (compare *primacy of Scripture*).

Heidelberg Catechism (1563). A formulation of Christian belief in the Reformed tradition, emphasizing God's grace and personal piety; a significant part of Phillip William Otterbein's theological background and part of the legacy of The United Brethren Church and its successor bodies.

Holiness. A term that Wesley used to describe the inward and outward righteousness that is given the faithful believer by God's grace in sanctification; often described as "faith working through love" (see Confession of Faith, XI).

Holy Communion. One of the principal means of grace, the sacramental act (Eucharist) whereby the Last Supper is remembered and our redemption is recalled. The body and blood of Christ are presented in the consecrated elements and received in faith, and the believer is strengthened and confirmed in the faith (see Articles of Religion, XVIII; Confession of Faith, VI).

Holy Spirit. The third person of the Trinity; the active presence of God through Christ in Creation and human history, comforting, convicting, redeeming, empowering, and sustaining the faithful (see Articles of Religion, IV; Confession of Faith, III).

Homilies. A series of sermonic essays (by Thomas Cranmer, John Jewel, and others) issued during the reigns of Edward VI and Elizabeth I to provide an official repository of Anglican doctrine through careful exposition of the Thirty-Nine Articles.

Incarnation. The embodiment of God's Word in flesh and blood in Jesus Christ, thereby fully identified with humanity in order to effect our salvation (see Articles of Religion, II; Confession of Faith, II).

Interfaith dialogue. Discussions between and among representatives of various religions of the world; distinguished from ecumenical dialogue among various Christian bodies.

Judicial Council. A group of nine persons elected by General Conference and responsible for ruling on questions of constitutionality in matters of church law and practice.

Justification. Pardon or forgiveness of sins by God's grace whereby the repentant believer is accepted as a child of God. Wesley's view stressed the necessity of faith as the sole immediate and direct condition of justification (*sola fide*), though good works are indirectly necessary, as true faith works through love.

Kingdom/reign of God. The present and future manifestation of the sovereignty of God, evident to some extent where God's love and justice prevail in human history, and fulfilled in the end time; a central theme of Jesus' teachings.

Laity. The people of God (*laos* means "people"). The term is traditionally applied to those members of the church who are not ordained (the clergy).

"Large Minutes." In British Methodism, a collection of the more significant doctrinal and disciplinary decisions (representing policies) from the Wesleyan conferences, revised in successive editions during the eighteenth century. The 1780 edition provided the basis for the American Methodist *Form of Discipline* first adopted at the Christmas Conference in 1785 (compare *Minutes*).

Means of grace. Those sacramental and devotional acts whereby the grace of God is especially mediated to humankind; by Wesley, sometimes called the ordinances of God (see *Discipline,* ¶ 68, General Rules, Rule 3).

Minutes. Reports of Wesleyan conferences in the form of questions and answers on matters of doctrine and discipline; in some cases reported statistics from across the movement, but also represented summaries of Wesley's views on important matters (compare *"Large Minutes"*).

Notes (Explanatory Notes Upon the New Testament). A version of the New Testament with commentary, published by John Wesley in 1755 as a guide for the Methodists in their use of the Bible; cited in the "Large Minutes" in 1763 as one of the Wesleyan standards of doctrine by which proper preaching could be judged.

Patristic teachings. The ideas of those leading Christian writers (*patres* means "fathers") who flourished during the first few centuries of the church and whose attempts to define and defend Christian doctrine provide evidence for the developing life and thought of the early church.

Pelagianism. The principal heresy proposing that salvation could be attained by human effort (good works), using only the divine grace given naturally to humankind; named for its main proponent, Pelagius, and condemned by Augustine; often associated (by its opponents) with works-righteousness in those who stress free will in their understanding of salvation.

Practical divinity. An approach to religious understanding and expression (typical of Wesley) that focuses on the practice (*praxis*) of Christianity, primarily the process of salvation and the manner of Christian living (discipleship), resulting in stress on soteriology and holiness.

Prevenient grace. The divine love that precedes (*prevenire* means "to come before") any conscious human impulse or action in the process of salvation; emphasized by Wesley to show that such human decisions by the faithful are always responsive to and enabled by God's grace.

Primacy of Scripture. The Protestant idea, consistently held by all Methodist traditions, that the Bible is the primary source of God's self-disclosing revelation of Christian truth. The interpretation of Scripture requires the guidance of the Holy Spirit and benefits from a constant attentiveness to recent scholarship as well as continual integration with the theological guidelines of tradition, experience, and reason.

Protestant. Those Christian bodies that trace their roots to the reforming traditions of the sixteenth century under Luther, Calvin, Zwingli, Cranmer, and others who attempted to reform the medieval Roman Catholic tradition but in fact contributed to the formation of new denominations.

Reason. The capacity to analyze and comprehend in rational ways, whether one is dealing with ideas or examining sensible data; essential to theological reflection and any attempt to articulate a comprehensive view of reality.

Regeneration/new birth. The result of God's forgiving love in justification whereby a person becomes a new creature (is born again) through the Holy Spirit; the beginning or threshold of sanctification; associated with baptism and with conversion (see Articles of Religion, XVII; Confession of Faith, VI).

Restrictive Rules. Six rules (adopted in 1808) that limit the powers of the General Conference; thereby viewed as providing the first constitutional statement of The Methodist Episcopal Church and still in effect today (see *Discipline*, ¶¶ 16–20 of the Constitution).

Sacraments. Rites ordained by Christ, outward signs of the Christian's profession of faith and of God's gracious love acting to strengthen and sustain the believer; understood in the Protestant traditions to be two in number, baptism and Holy Communion (see also *means of grace*).

Sanctification. The process and point of growth in grace whereby faithful believers actually become more holy in the sense of having "the love of God shed abroad in their hearts by the Holy Spirit"; reached not simply by effort but by constant attentiveness to God's grace, with the goal of manifesting perfect love or "entire sanctification" or Christian perfection (see Confession of Faith, XI).

Scriptural holiness. Wesley's term for sanctification, the spread of which he saw as the reason for God's having raised up the Methodists.

Sermons on Several Occasions. A collection of Wesley's published sermons, eventually comprising nine volumes, that contain what he viewed as "the essentials of true religion." The volumes that had been published by 1763 were specified by the "Large Minutes" of that year as one of the standard measures of pure Methodist preaching; they contain the distinctive doctrines of Wesleyan Methodism.

Social gospel. A form of Christian life and thought that stresses societal responsibility, both in terms of the causes of social problems and the implementation of God's reign on earth; compatible with Wesley's social concerns, the movement began to flourish among Methodists in the late nineteenth century.

Social Principles. The official statement of United Methodist positions on social issues; derived from the "Social Creed" first adopted in 1908 and subject to revision only by the General Conference (see *Discipline,* Part III).

Socinianism. One of the Reformation heresies that denied the divinity of Christ and the doctrine of the Trinity; named from its chief proponent, Fausto Sozzini (Socinus), who encouraged a moderate form of Unitarianism.

Sunday Service. Wesley's abridgement of the Book of Common Prayer, done "for the Methodists in North America"; accepted by the Christmas Conference in 1784 but largely ignored in subsequent liturgical developments in American Methodism.

Theology. Critical and constructive reflection on the teaching and practice of the church, including its doctrine. Theology is an instrument for the church's continual renewal in faithfulness to its mission (compare *doctrine*).

Tradition. The Christian tradition is the continuing activity of God's Spirit in human activity, the historical legacy of those communities of faith that share in this transforming work, and the continuing process by which various formulations and practices are passed on to successive generations.

Trinity. The central concept of the orthodox Christian doctrine of God, the three persons of the Trinity expressed in traditional terms as "Father, Son, and Holy Spirit," an essential unity that is also manifest in a variety of creative, redemptive, and sustaining actions in human history.